Life in Japan

*Understanding the Culture,
Knowing the Rules*

*What You Need to Know About Living
in Japan*

DINGO
BOOK CLUB

"Great Books Change Life"

© Copyright 2018 by Dingo Publishing - All rights reserved.

The contents of this book may not be reproduced, duplicated or transmitted without direct written permission from the author.

Under no circumstances will any legal responsibility or blame be held against the publisher for any reparation, damages, or monetary loss due to the information herein, either directly or indirectly.

Legal Notice:

You cannot amend, distribute, sell, use, quote or paraphrase any part or the content within this book without the consent of the author.

Disclaimer Notice:

Please note the information contained within this document is for educational and entertainment purposes only. No warranties of any kind are expressed or implied. Readers acknowledge that the author is not engaging in the rendering of legal, financial, medical or professional advice. Please consult a licensed professional before attempting any techniques outlined in this book.

By reading this document, the reader agrees that under no circumstances are is the author responsible for any losses, direct or indirect, which are incurred as a result of the use of information contained within this document, including, but not limited to, —errors, omissions, or inaccuracies.

Table of Contents

Introduction 6

Chapter 1: History of Japan 8

    Major Economics 13

    Fitness and Work 14

Chapter 2: Culture of Japan 16

    Three Japanese Culture 16

        Ainu 18

        Ryukyuan 21

        Yamato 23

    Examining the Samurai 25

    Geisha 26

    Kimonos 29

    Japanese Gardens 30

    Japanese Tea Ceremonies 34

    Japanese Language and Dialect 36

Chapter 3: Lifestyle 38

    The Diet 40

    Entertainment 42

    Exercise 44

    Bathing 45

    Tea as a Staple 45

- Chapter 4: Housing Options 46
  - Average Rental Prices 46
  - Types of Housing 48
  - Living Patterns 51
- Chapter 5: Transportation 52
  - Trains 52
  - Air Travel 55
  - Buses 55
  - Ferries 56
  - Car Rental 56
- Chapter 6: Weather 57
  - Average Temperatures Per Month 57
- Chapter 7: Jobs and Cost of Living 60
  - Cost of Living Explanation 60
  - Schooling 62
  - Jobs for Expats 63
- Chapter 8: Best and Worst 65
  - The Best 65
  - The Worst 67
  - Etiquette and Customs 68
- Conclusion 70
- Before you go 72

More books from us 74
Bonus 78

Introduction

Japan may be one of the smaller countries, set on an island, but it has a diverse culture, a dominant financial center, and long, varied history. Japan is 145,932 square miles in size. As globalization grows, more people become fascinated with life in Japan, its past, and the pop culture. Manga, Anime, Sony PlayStation, and so much more has become highly desirable by people around the world. It is little wonder that a book about the history, culture, lifestyle, and living in Japan is necessary to explore all that such a tiny country offers.

From a time of some of the most significant warriors ever known to the tumultuous period during the World Wars to now, Japan has shown the world that it is possible to be small and succeed.

Whether you are interested in the culture of Japan, the rules and language or more of the way of life one can enjoy on the island; it will all be available.

In the end, you are going to understand the best and worst of Japanese living, as well as if you can afford to move there and enjoy the history, diverse landscape, and people of the island.

You are going to fall in love with Japan, perhaps hate it a little sometimes. You will be able to enjoy a vacation or live there, confidently knowing you have explored all you can in written form before arriving.

Chapter 1:
History of Japan

The history of Japan would take a book itself; however, it is possible to give a short introduction to the periods in history. These eras are listed:

1. Early Japan
2. Nara and Heian
3. Kamakura
4. Muromachi
5. Azuchi-Momoyama
6. Edo
7. Meiji
8. Taisho and Early Showa
9. Postwar

Early Japan is up until 710 AD. The second period ends in 1192, with the Kamakura period ending in 1333. The Muromachi era lasted until 1573, with the Azuchi-Momoyama a short thirty-year affair. Edo is perhaps the most well known as it is often depicted in shows and movies

(1603 to 1868). The Meiji ended in 1912 when the Taisho and Early Showa took over between 1912 and 1945. Today, Japan is said to be in Postwar.

Some of the critical elements of Japan are the Jomon, who is the first Japanese to live from 300 BC on, becoming the Yamato, Ainu, and Ryukyuan. Rice was introduced in 300 to 250 BC as an essential staple.

Tombs were first erected from 250 BC to 538 AD, during a time known as Kofun.

In early Japan, during the Asuka timeframe, Buddhism was introduced from China, and the seventeen articles of the Shotoku Constitution were designed.

Nara was the first Capital of Japan, which was established in 710, but only 74 years later, the capital was relocated to Nagaoka. During the Nara and Heian period, the capital moved again to what is now Kyoto. Power changes also occurred where the Taira Kiyomori clan took over political decisions. It was also a time when the Jodo Sect of Buddhism was formed, and the Minamoto clan ended the Taira leadership.

Zen Buddhism began in 1191, and the government would change a few more times, giving rise to the legal code called

Joei Shikimoku. Mongols also tried to invade Japan in between 1274 and 1281.

For a small period during the Muromachi period, there were southern and northern leaders, due to a fight in which the emperor fled to Yoshino in southern Japan. However, before the 1300s was over the two courts were unified again. The Portuguese sailed to Japan in the 1500s, introducing Christianity and firearms. It is also the century when Nobunaga rose to power as one of the most revered Samurai.

Japan tried to invade Korea during 1592 to 1598 but was unsuccessful. There were also plenty of warring states in Japan, with the fall of Hojo and Tokugawa defeating rivals at Sekigahara.

During the Edo period, the Tokugawa government was in power in the new capital of Edo, or what is now Tokyo. Christianity was persecuted, and one shogunate clan was wiped out when Osaka Castle was seized.

Japan was extremely isolated during this time, eliminating a lot of trade with Korea and China. They also closed their borders to Western travelers. Many Koreans became enslaved if they tried to enter Japan without the proper documentation. Towards the late 1700s, Russia started negotiating trade and finally, Commodore Matthew Perry forced Japan to open ports for trade.

The Meiji Era was a time of great feats and war. In 1872, the first railway built, running between Tokyo and Yokohama. The Sino-Japanese and Russo-Japanese wars occurred, and there was the annexation of Korea in 1910.

Japan became part of the allied forces in 1910 during World War I. After the war, Tokyo and Yokohama had to recover from the Great Kanto Earthquake.

During the Showa period, the Manchurian incident occurs, with the second Sino-Japanese war starting six years later. The Second World War began, with Japan on the opposite side, instead of backing their moves to destroy the US, with Pearl Harbor's destruction. It was a period when hate was definitely abundant, with Japan trying to win, killing thousands, and winding up surrendering after two atomic bombs destroyed Nagasaki and Hiroshima. Until 1952, there was an allied occupation of Japan, and four years later the country joined the UN. Relations with China become normalized in 1972, and a year then there was an oil crisis.

However, during the later 1900s, Japan started producing many electronics, cars, and other items desired by Western countries. It helped Japan rise as a financial power, being listed in the top five countries.

Throughout their history have been earthquakes, Tsunamis, and devastating choices in wars. But, Japan is continuing their financial domination exporting more than they import, keeping the budget on the positive side instead of a deficit. Their trade relations are also better for oil needs.

This is not to say that Japan has not suffered some financial setbacks, but they do continue to show intelligence in how they regulate the foreign currency market and banking system.

The US continues to keep military relations with Japan, although, there are some negative thoughts about keeping a US base on Okinawa. Talk in the most recent century was asking for the US to leave or at least dwindle their numbers, but a resurgent problem with North Korea and its nuclear weapon program has again changed these talks.

Japan and South Korea continue to run war simulations together to show their power as a means of controlling actions by North Korea.

Major Economics

Japan is the third largest auto industry and holds a high ranking for innovative global patent filings. In 2015, Japan held an estimated $13.5 trillion in financial assets and 54 of the Fortune Global 500 companies. Japan keeps much of their financial assets in the private sector, which also affects the countries wealth and caste system. Regarding the GDP, Japan has the highest ranking of public debt, with the national debt predominately in the private sector.

Japan has gone nuclear-free, regarding power plants, switching to natural gas. The country also depends mostly on rail transport. About 84% of Japan's energy is imported from other countries, but they are looking towards hydroelectricity for renewable energy and lowering their dependency on other countries.

For industries, manufacturing, real estate, and wholesale/retail trade are the highest percentages providing the GDP numbers. Other services and activities, such as agriculture and tourism, are the top category.

Fitness and Work

Japan has worked to increase the health of their people by offering better working environments, despite the long hours. Many industries in Tokyo, require workers to remain on the clock for twelve hours, with the first 20 to 40 hours of overtime going unpaid. The work culture has usually been for long hours, but many are beginning to fight this when their contract states eight hour days. Japanese people grow up with the thought that they will have 100 hour work weeks, but in saying this, there are compromises with longer holiday allowances.

Companies are also adding in ways to help their office employees remain physically active, such as the treadmill desks and providing rooftop gardens. These are not always provided, but they are becoming more normal.

The correlation between work hours and pay is sometimes skewed. For example, a pilot can earn $143,000 or 17,121,000 yen. They usually work 138 hours in a month. A medical doctor working 174 hours earns closer to 11,540,000 yen, so less than a pilot. Jobs such as crane workers, nurses, and factory workers work anywhere from 170 to 200 hours for as little as 4,000,000 yen or $35,680.

So, the history of overworking employees, from the earliest of times until now, is that many are working long hours, but their culture does not complain. They know what they are accepting when they take an offer, and it is imperative for them to choose a job they will love or have temporarily.

Chapter 2:
Culture of Japan

Japanese culture is varied from what many Western countries understand. A great deal of what we think we know comes from pop culture, and to a degree, it is accurately depicted. However, once you visit Japan and live among the people there, you will see the diversity and the belief that life can be enjoyable, as well as filled with challenging work.

Not everything in Japan is perfect of course, but there are certainly lessons that can be gained from the current culture.

Starting with pop culture, some people walk around with their hair painted assorted colors, such as blue or red to pay homage to their favorite anime or manga. But, everyday life is generally filled with long work hours and an eye towards fitness.

To understand the culture of Japan, it is better to look at the past and work our way to the modern aspects you will see on a visit to the country.

Three Japanese Culture

Japanese culture includes Samurai, Geisha, Japanese gardens, tea ceremonies, and kimonos. The culture has roots in Chinese culture, but historically, there have always been differences between the two due to the land mass separation. Japan also enjoyed extended periods of isolation prior to their enforced segregation later. Certain aspects of China were imported, overwhelming the Japanese with Chinese culture, but it did not take long for a distinctly Japanese style to arrive, which is often seen the gardens and temples.

It is imperative you understand that there are three distinct cultures in Japan and it is offensive to lump everyone into "Japanese." Like "Westerners" have diversity, Japan has primarily three cultural groups: Ainu, Ryukyuan, and Yamato.

Ainu

The Ainu, pronounced Aynu, are indigenous to Northern Honshu, Hokkaido, and a few islands north of Hokkaido. There are genetic differences between Ainu, Ryukyuan, and Yamato.

When it comes to religion, the Ainu follow distinctly different concepts than Buddhism and Shinto. They still worship gods, as if they are elements of nature. The Ainu also have animal and plant gods.

In the 1700s, when the cultures of Japan started mixing, it was clear to see differences in the clothing worn by the Ainu versus Yamato and Ryukyuan. The housing choices also differed, with bark, grasses, and bamboo used to construct their homes. Houses were seven by five meters, which is approximately 23 by 16 feet.

The Ainu are primarily isolated today, preferring to keep to themselves much as they did in the past. A CNN travel piece says some guides work at a museum, but they are wary of tourists and typically quiet sharing only a little about their heritage. Some Ainu live on Sakhalin, near the east coast of Russia and in Honshu, which is Japan's largest island.

Estimates put about 24,000 Ainu people living in the world today. Their language is a mixture of native and Japanese, with only about ten people still speaking fluent native Ainu language.

The Ainu are known for their brutal hunting methods of animals. They still revere bears and wolves, but hunting is normal. Deer are also a significant source of meat for them. The fact is—Ainu use techniques from their past to hunt, which can be against most of the worlds animal rights.

This area of Japan was harsh for a living, and it still is. The Japanese government did not recognize the Ainu as indigenous to Japan until this century. The ten-year anniversary of recognition is in 2018.

Still, between 1868 and 1912, there was a movement of a more global Japan. This period is referred to as the Meiji Era when mainstream Japanese heritage was more integrated with the distinct cultures like the Ainu.

Education is critical to raising awareness of the Ainu, and it is said that the Ainu cultural center in Tokyo will be ready for the 2020 Olympic Games. Inside the new facility, people will be able to learn about the traditional dress of the Ainu people, their hunting methods, and struggles to live in a modern world. It is not to say that there are no current buildings in Northern Japan; however, there are still traditions followed that come together to create an exciting landscape.

Ryukyuan

The Ryukyuan live mostly on the islands of Okinawa and the Ryukyu islands. There are also some northern islands they inhabit. There are numerous sub-groups of Ryukyuan's including Okinawans, Amamians, Yonagunians, Yaeyamans, and Miyakoans. Each of these groups has specific dialects. Like the Ainu, Ryukyuan people have distinct religious beliefs, architecture, and clothing. Their clothing is not as different from mainstream Japanese as the Ainu.

There was the Ryukyuan Kingdom that was taken by Satsuma in the 17th century. The Ryukyuan culture spread throughout more of Japan due to the overthrowing of the kingdom, but lately, genetic studies place Ryukyuan and Ainu as more genetically linked than the Yamato. The Ainu are stocky, fairer, and have Caucasian elements.

It is also known that the Ryukyuan had ties with China before the Japanese colonization of the Meiji Period.

With regards to religion, the Ryukyuan follow traditions and legends that relate to ancestor worship, meaning they respect the living, dead, gods, and spirits, with a little worship of animals. There is influence from Chinese religions, including Taoism, Buddhism, and Confucianism. Ryukyuan has in some instances adopted the mainstream Shinto religion. One of the ancient aspects of the Ryukyuan religion is their onarigami belief, which is the spiritual superiority of females. They believed in priestesses or the Noro system. It is a system derived from the Amamikyu. Many of the shamans and mediums were female.

Yamato

The most dominant culture of Japan is the Yamato people. About 98% of the population is genetically linked to the Yamato. It was not until the 1800s that the term Yamato Japanese was used to show the distinctions between the three-distinct people of Japan. It was related to the incorporation of the Empire of Japan, with the Yamato Dynasty running the Imperial house from 660 BC. The Yamato people have ruled in each of the significant dynasties, periods, and kingdoms of Japan.

As the world continues to find the primary origin of "humans," archeologist do believe Japanese people were on the island before the formulation of Chinese and Korean cultures. However, it is not a concrete theory. There are definite differences between Japan, China, and Korea, but also enough to show that hunter-gatherers migrated to the island from northern and southern Asian locations.

For the Yamato, Buddhism was the primary religion, and it continues to be the same today. They are also responsible for building the tomb culture for the aristocracy during the early Kofun cultural period.

It is the Yamato who adapted to the changes in the world, starting with hunting, gathering, and fishing, they also adopted technologies from other parts of the world through trade to encourage innovations.

Examining the Samurai

Part of the history and culture of Japan are the Samurai. The term was first applied to written works in the 900s; however, it is known that warriors existed prior to this time. The Asuka and Nara periods, which coincide with Tang China and Silla in the 660s, are when Japan required military reform. The Taiho Code of 702 AD was formed as part of the restructuring of the military to create a military that would be able to fight. Emperor Monmu also established a law during these periods that 1 in 3 to 4 males would be drafted into the military. They would need to bring their weapons but would be exempt from taxes and duties.

The rise of the Samurai is marked by the late Heian period, around 1160 AD. Samurai fought in a naval battle showing their prowess. But, it was Emperor Kanmu who established the title of Shogun in the 8th century or the early Heian Period.

Geisha

While talking of groups of people, the Geisha is also a necessary discussion on the culture of Japan.

Many myths are surrounding the concept of Geisha, perpetuated by pop culture such as the movie *Memoirs of a Geisha*. The Geisha is a woman, who follow a distinct line of discipline, beauty, and grace. The word "geisha" translates as an artisan or performing artist, but it is meant to indicate a high-class professional, trained in traditional entertainment. Geisha attend to guests at banquets, parties, and meals often demonstrating their skills with the shamisen. They are meant to initiate games, conversation, and more. Usually, they serve in tea houses, ryotei (traditional restaurants), and are paid a fee.

It may surprise you to learn—the first geisha were men. They started working in the 18th century, and it was not until later than females began occupying the position of geisha. In the 18th century some geisha did start offering sex as part of the entertainment; however, the oiran geisha became less popular and Japanese men began asking for a high-class companion there to act as hostess instead of a more intimate friend.

So, if someone says geisha are prostitutes it is more accurate to say they are oiran and geishas are highly-skilled entertainers who go through a great deal of training. Geisha did have personal relationships with patrons, but today the tradition is to be separate from their danna regarding a more intimate relationship. They are there for financial reasons to be hostesses. In the past, it is possible young girls were sold to geisha houses (okiya) for reasons of poverty; however, today all geisha make it a career choice.

Geisha do primarily make their money by being hostesses for men or mostly male-dominated parties; however, working in restaurants, they also provide care for women. It should also be understood that the mizuage is a ceremony that was performed by courtesans and prostitutes in the past, but it did not involve the maiko, which is apprentice geishas. Maiko is young, starting training at 15, 16, or 18 depending on where a person lives.

Geisha do have specific hairstyles, ornaments, makeup, and dress that they follow. The traditional clothing is the kimono. The makeup is a full white face for maiko only. Geisha only wear makeup in an exceptional performance. The hair ornaments are meant to be decorative, with simple combs or kanzashi ornaments. The hair is highly skilled, using wigs to provide the elegant styles. However, many geishas are turning to natural hairstyles like the maiko trainees due to hair loss. The last part of the costumes is the footwear, which is usually high wooden sandals for maiko and shorter wooden sandals or geta for the geishas.

While the tradition was once prevalent, many of the geisha work and live in Kyoto, but it is harder to find people in Tokyo performing in this position. About 1,000 to 2,000 women are currently working as geisha throughout Japan. The exact number is difficult to pin down due to a lack of study in the small cities. Kyoto shows an employment of possibly 300. It is also hard to pin down the number since some are a maiko, studying to work as artisans, but may not follow through with the same high-class artistry as the "geisha." Training has opened for non-Japanese who wish to learn the discipline and principles of the geisha. Maiko can also be taken into work as a helper, doing errands, but unless they make a formal public debut, they will not be "official."

Kimonos

It should not surprise you that what we take for granted as traditional Japanese clothing, to epitomize the culture of Japan, was just the word for "clothing." The style of Kimono that we recognize as the conventional geisha dress was the way they made clothing in the late 700s AD. As clothing making became more developed the style of apparel increased. At first, separate upper and lower garments were constructed, as were one-piece outfits to ensure a person was thoroughly covered and warm.

Adding layers to clothing started in the 12th century, where bright colors were added to represent different classes. Now what we know as the kimono is worn for special occasions like funerals, weddings, tea ceremonies, as a matter of employment in entertainment fields.

Japanese Gardens

Japanese Gardens are part of Japanese art, and they have taken on a life of their own around the world. Numerous cities across the globe and the USA, in particular, are creating Japanese Gardens to bring the culture, heritage, and relaxation of these landscapes to the people. Many cities hire renowned Japanese artists to provide all the elements a garden should have.

Historic Japanese gardens are spread throughout Kyoto and Tokyo. The difference is that many of the gardens in Kyoto will also have shrines and historic temples. They even change with the seasons, with colorful foliage in the fall and beautiful Sakura blossoms in spring.

Two things go into these heritage sites: time and nature. It takes time for the gardens to grow naturally, with little help from the caretakers. Japanese gardens usually symbolize gravel or sand to show rivers, while other rocks are meant to depict mountains.

Japanese merchants during the Asuka period (538 to 710) would visit China, bringing back Chinese arts, including gardens. Buddhist monks continued with this tradition, as did diplomats, scholars, translator, and students. The gardens first appeared in the 7th century.

The oldest style is called Paradise, and it was created during the Heian period. The Sakuteiki is a book written on the tradition about the Japanese technique and still revered today.

With the flourishing Zen Buddhism belief during 1185 to 1573, the concept of the Zen garden was produced. Zen Buddhist temples incorporate this style. There are specific elements that make it a Japanese garden of any persuasion, including Zen.

- Water
- Gravel
- Sand
- Stone
- Island
- Rock
- Hills
- Teahouse
- Stream
- Fish

- Bridge
- Strolling paths
- Stone lanterns
- Bamboo pipes
- Flowers
- Moss
- Ponds
- Trees
- Gates
- Statues
- Garden architecture
- Garden Fences
- Water basin

As long as some of these elements or all of them are found in a garden, it is considered a Japanese Garden.

Like the cultural differences between races, there are also three main types of Japanese gardens: Karensansui (Zen), Tsukiyama and Chaniwa.

The Zen Garden is a spiritual location, with sand or gravel representing the sea or river, rocks to show mountains and islands, and few small trees. It is a place for yoga, meditation, or just observing the patterns made in the gravel.

The Tsukiyama is a hill and pond garden, filled with the lush mossy landscape, complete with water, bridges, fish, trees, stones, hills, flowers, and small plants.

The Chaniwa is the tea garden often accompanied by a tea ceremony house. There is an inner and outer garden, with a covered gate, lantern style figures, and water basin or tsukubai for washing your hands. There are also stepping stones in the tea garden.

There are other non-traditional gardens, like the newer courtyard garden. These gardens allow current people of Japan to have a little place to relax and enjoy nature, with their favorite elements.

Japanese Tea Ceremonies

The Japanese Tea Ceremony is an essential element of traditional culture. It can be called Chanoyu, Ocha, or Sado. It is a ritual ceremony preparing and serving Matcha, and traditional Japanese sweets. Preparing the tea has predefined movements throughout, including how to pour the tea in front of someone. It is not about drinking the tea, so much as it is about the aesthetics, preparation, and the feelings of one's heart. The host has to consider the guest with each movement and gesture. The tea utensils are placed at specific angles for the guest's viewpoint.

Tea was first brought into Japan during the 600s AD. However, it was in the eighth century that a formal ceremony was created. Japan was somewhat forced into the building and cultivating their traditions around tea because of its rare and valuable connotations. Tea was challenging to get at first, with China holding on to their seeds and the nobility preventing lower class people from gaining it as a regular beverage.

The ceremony adapted overtime, with a Zen Buddhist erecting a temple and serving tea as part of the religious purposes of the location. He also suggested that the leaves be ground before adding the water. Later Hui Tsung, a Sung emperor, mentioned the addition of a bamboo whisk to stir the leaves. Grinding the leaves and using a whisk are two necessary elements to the ceremony you will see in tea houses throughout the world, and particularly in Japan.

The qualities of a proper server are those who have faith in the performance of the tea, who act with decorum befitting a master, and those who have practical, excellent skills.

Japanese Language and Dialect

Japanese has dialects, which helps others pinpoint the region a person may be from, as it does in any country. The origins of the language are unknown but thought to be rooted in the Altaic language family, like Turkish, Mongolian and other Asian systems. There are also some similarities in Austronesian languages, notably, Polynesian.

Writing Japanese varies by the character sets. There are three: Kanji, Hiragana, and Katakana. When writing Japanese, one can write in horizontal rows from the top to the bottom of the page or in traditional style creating vertical columns, going right to left on the page.

Grammar for Japanese is simple, without too many gender articles or plural/singular concepts. However, there are some conjugation rules for verbs and adjectives.

Pronunciation is how the language makes its mark. Japan has few sounds, which makes it easier to learn. There are also fewer homonyms, in which words are pronounced in the same way, but have different meanings. In Chinese, you would find one word can mean more than two things.

The important aspect about Japanese is the level of speech you use. It is necessary to use honorific language or Keigo when you are in formal situations. As a Westerner, you would be expected to use formal language and rules versus talking like a friend or you would to a child.

Chapter 3:
Lifestyle

In Japanese history overview, it was clear to see that employment is a significant factor in the Japanese lifestyle. According to some news reports, people sleep perhaps 35 hours a week and work around 100 hours. It makes it difficult to understand how such a culture, who seems to live only for work, can have a lifestyle.

It is precisely the work ethic that demands a view of a lifestyle that completely separates the Japanese and many Asian cultures from Western countries. Yes, work takes up most of the time, but there are other benefits, such as company meals, fitness during working hours, and fun.

Are there some downsides—yes—rumors and studies show issues with mental distress. But, then again, one has to consider if all the facts are supplied. The cultures of Japan view depression and other mental health issues with different stereotypes than Western cultures, even to how they see suicide. Thankfully, recent studies are showing that mental health needs to be more mainstream regarding correcting it, and the country is slowly moving out of the dark ages. Unfortunately, there is still a stigma about mental illness, even depression that prevents people from seeking help. For suicide, on a global scale, Japan has one of the worst problems.

Perhaps, it can be argued that if you work long hours, despite some of the nicest working conditions and amenities, you still feel the weight of the world on your shoulders.

For tourists, it may be easier to look at what Japan can teach us about living longer, healthier lives, as studies show many Asian cultures do in comparison to Western countries. For people who want to live and work in Japan—you will need to change your viewpoint on what it means to work.

The Diet

Japan is heavily invested in seafood diets. The National Marine Fisheries Service shows 55.7 kilograms per capita of seafood was consumed in 2016. In comparison, the US ate 24.2 kilograms. People who eat a lot of fish tend to live healthier lifestyles because there are different cholesterol levels in fish versus meat. In fact, there is a 35 percent lower risk of heart disease in people who eat fish as a primary protein. Omega 3 fatty acids are linked to several types of cancers, which shows that fish can help prevent these issues, as well as inflammation. Some studies prove eating fish can enhance the mood due to obtaining Omega-3 fatty acids.

Another aspect of the Japanese diet that helps with a healthier lifestyle is seaweed. The UN numbers show 100,000 tons of seaweed is eaten each year by Japanese people, with 20 different species used in their cuisine. Seaweed can offer 2 to 9 grams of protein per cup. Seaweed is also known to regulate estrogen and estradiol levels, helping to reduce breast cancer in woman.

Japanese cuisine is centered on seafood, raw and cooked, okonomiyaki, noodle dishes, and chicken. Japan is also reputed to have better beef, Kobe.

Fermentation, of food, is another favorite part of the Japanese diet. Several of the side dishes offered on menus are pickled. Soy sauce, miso, and natto are also helpful in keeping one health since it helps with one's digestion. Adding miso paste to your cooking can help break down food before it reaches your lips, thus giving rise to a better immune system.

Entertainment

Japan is big on entertainment. Karaoke is one of the top pastimes for Japanese. There are at least 229 locations for Karaoke in Japan for just one chain, Big Echo. Around 20,000 men sing and go drinking with friends after work, and they show an improvement in cardiovascular health versus those who do not go out singing.

Overall, entertainment is a big industry in Japan. There are various bars, with and without karaoke, and company meals are part of the package. Social support is tremendous for most people working and living in Japan, not only as a way to build better teams in a working environment but also to keep healthier.

Whether, you enjoy manga, anime, or games, studies are also showing that letting your inner "fun" person out is going to do you good. Japan takes this as serious as they do their long work hours by offering clubs, for gaming and dressing up as characters.

Another aspect of the Japanese lifestyle is laughing and being silly. A lot of the shows, including drama and reality television productions, are incredibly, over-the-top silly. They also offer commercials, Westerners find silly, but the studies come back with laughter being a good dose of medicine. Laughter is known to release endorphins that reduce pain, alleviate depression, and increase one's immune system. If you live in Japan, be prepared to see silly things you might consider "stupid," and yet find you cannot help but watch. You cannot be serious all the time; especially, working 80 plus hour weeks.

Exercise

Keeping fit is an essential part of the lifestyle. Not only are fitness options provided at work, but there are places for yoga, meditation, and relaxation too, which keeps people energized.

Japan provided a 16th national holiday called Mountain Day. It celebrates mountain climbing and helps bring the concept of forest therapy alive. Forest therapy is exactly what it sounds like—going out in the green forests around the cities and enjoying nature, recuperating and exercising. Being outdoors, helps people gain vitamin D, which is necessary for energy. Not getting enough vitamin D is known to lead to autoimmune disorders, cancers, and arthritis. By spending time outdoors in quiet forests, researchers show a 20 to 50 percent improvement in cognitive function.

It is not a bad way to look at the Japanese lifestyle and know you want to take part in it. Being healthier, simply by living more like the people of Japan is a possibility.

Bathing

Japan is also reputed to have some of the best baths in the world. A part of the lifestyle is the public baths and hot springs. About 85 percent of Japanese people spend their end of the day in a bath. During the 17th century, numerous written texts expounded on the reasons for a hot soak to stop illness. There is something to this line of thinking, since baths, particularly in hot springs, are full of minerals that help with skin disorders, rheumatism, and neuralgia. Those who meditate during baths also see a drop in blood pressure.

Tea as a Staple

Japanese citizens also make tea a part of their lifestyle. No, you do not have to have a tea ceremony every day, but just make tea. Drinking five cups of green tea per day can lower mortality by 26 percent, according to one study. There are also correlations with improved cognitive function and reduced heart disease risk.

Chapter 4:
Housing Options

Before you think about housing and whether you can afford to live in Japan, you have to understand the exchange rate. For one yen, you obtain 0.0089 USD. In opposites terms, for 1 USD, you gain 112.11 Yen. The yen is structured in a way that it is in the 100ths instead of singular. It does not mean it is a boon of money. Now, keep in mind the exchange rate changes over time. You always have to check the current rate for the time you are visiting or living in Japan to know whether it is more in your favor or not.

To help you, if you are paying 82,922.00 Yen for an apartment, you are going to pay around $740 per month for rent. If your monthly salary is half that amount, it is not a job paying you much at all. Going forward, just remember the exchange rate, so you can decide if you are living in an affordable location.

Average Rental Prices

If you live in the city center, you can expect your rent to be around $740 per month for a one-bedroom apartment. Those who live in one-bedroom residences outside of the city will pay close to $500 per month. Three-bedroom units are

169,580 and 100,879 Yen for the town and out of the city, respectively. When you compare three-bedroom units to some of the more expensive units in the towns in the US, $1500 for one month is not that bad. According to real estate analytical studies, rent is 33% lower in the cities of Japan compared to the significant world and US cities like New York.

Buying a home, an apartment is priced per square footage. You can expect to pay close to $1500 per square foot inside the city and $450 per square foot outside of the city. These are all averages. There are certainly places that are more or less expensive, with a range of 55 to 280,000 Yen rentals and 27,870 to 176,514 for purchase.

Types of Housing

Japan has modern and traditional styles of housing. Contemporary structures are predominantly taking over the city, with a few single-family detached and multi-unit buildings. Some of the homes are individually owned, and others are under a corporation. Apartments can be tenant or owner-occupied.

Unmarried people can live in boarding houses, dorms, or barracks. One unique aspect of Japanese housing is that many are thought to have a limited lifespan, which means they are torn down and rebuilt every twenty or so years. For example, wooden structures are torn down after two decades, and concrete structures are demolished after thirty years.

Traditional homes are built without specific designations. Aside from the entrance, kitchen, bathroom, and toilet, all other rooms can become what one needs them to be, such as having one room that is living, dining, study, and bedroom, or switching the use of the rooms based on need.

The different living areas are separated by sliding doors, much like the modern offices in Japan. The doors can be made of wood and paper like Shoji screens or glass to provide more separation and insulation. Most of the doors are portable to move them around as necessary.

Modern structures are different. They may include more modern things such as doors and windows like Westerners are used to. Apaato or apartment buildings are a few stories in height, without a secure central entrance. The doors are accessed via balcony entrances for each unit. Mansion style homes are more elaborate with primary entrances, postboxes, and secure communal gates. They are also more sturdy in their construction than apaato buildings, which is why they are more expensive.

Some mansions are one-room or studio apartments, with a small bathroom. Laundry is also included, but only a washing machine. Wet articles of clothing are hung to dry, but one can add a dryer if it is affordable. A lot of people use laundry mats, sleep without beds, and use mats with comforters and pillows for their sleeping quarters.

Heating is typically kerosene, gas, or electric, with units set up in each room or moved about to keep occupied rooms warm. A lot of the time the heating units leave with the resident who is vacating the space. Traditional buildings do not use insulation, and it may not be in the low-budget apartments. Windows are also single-pane. Newer structures will have better options, such as insulated glazing on the windows, and insulation in the walls.

There are housing regulations in Japan, but you want to make certain when you buy if you buy that you are getting a building that is not old enough to be torn down. You also want to go over the regulations to learn the differences and make sure you are buying something with your money that is reasonable.

Living Patterns

Japanese culture is similar to the rest of Asia, in that living with your parents after you are an adult is acceptable. Most single people 20 to 34 live with their parents. Even after marriage, the couple will decide to live with one set of parents, often the male's parents. The change in tradition is more houses are becoming "two-generation" with a separate living quarters for the older couple and younger couple. Often, the communal areas bind the house together.

In the cities, unmarried couples are starting to live with each other. However, there is always the tradition that the elderly will live with their children when it becomes necessary. Elderly care facilities are not as much in demand, so people live at home with caretakers when necessary or have their children see to their needs.

Apartment sharing is a rare thing among friends and singles. But, with socioeconomic and demographic changes, this tradition is starting to change. There are some young people sharing apartments in the city for affordability reasons.

Chapter 5: Transportation

Japan's primary transportation system is the rail. The system offers public transportation between the major metropolitan areas and large cities. It is known for its superb service, punctuality, and the thousands using it.

For tourists and long-term visitors, it is helpful to understand the railway system, so you get on the correct path. However, there are still car and airplane options.

Trains

The Shinkansen is the high-speed train or bullet train that will get you from one point to the next as quickly as possible, with a regard for safety. Other trains provide transportation around the cities and different prefectures, but at a slower pace, stopping at more places and ensuring all workers can get where they need to go.

Night trains are also available. These trains go between the distant prefectures, allowing people to sleep in private areas while they travel.

You will want to examine the timetables and ticket options before coming to Japan. There are different rail passes, including an unlimited, nationwide pass that is for tourists. You can also choose the Seishun 18 Kippu, which is for local unlimited train travel versus entire country travel.

When you decide to take the train, you need to look at local, rapid, express, limited express, and super express as these are the categories that differentiate the number of stops and areas you can travel.

Seat categories include ordinary and green, with green being first class. Most trains have ordinary cars, but if you are going on a longer route, you will find green cars are less packed, with spacious seating, and 30 to 50 percent more expensive. The Shinkansen and limited express are non-reserved and reserved, but there are few reserved options.

Additionally, smoking cars are part of the long-distance train options, and on all other trains, smoking is prohibited. At first, when buying tickets you may want to seek a ticket booth, but once you get used to everything, some machines are available to help you figure out your routes. You just need to find the destination on the fare map, punch in which destination and insert the money or IC card.

Signage in the terminals is in Japanese and English unless you go to out of the way locations that are not typically popular with tourists. The most critical signs will always be in English and Japanese, such as exit and emergency.

Train etiquette requires that you do not block the door at stations, even when the trains are packed and that you place your items in the racks or on the floor near the seats, out of the walking path. Passengers tend to sleep, read, or use mobile devices when traveling. Talking on mobile phones is forbidden inside the trains. It is seen as rude.

Air Travel

There are international and domestic flights, as well as discount air tickets available, frequently. The major airports are Narita, Haneda, Kansai, Itami, Central Japan, New Chitose, Kobe, Komatsu, and Shizuoka. Most international passengers fly into Narita or Haneda, but they can also use Osaka's destinations. For travelers going to Okinawa, there are international flights.

Buses

The bus is for long distance and short distance. Unlike, the trains, buses are often not a way of travel for Japanese. However, for travelers, they can be perfect for the long-distance trip from one prefecture to another. Buses may also be used for the short commute from apartment to work when it is more affordable or more straightforward to do so. A lot of the system is used in smaller cities, where train travel is set for long-distance versus stopping at the principal streets.

Ferries

Japan's system for gaining access to the smaller islands is the ferry. It is cost-effective in comparison to domestic flights, and some islands may not offer domestic flights that fit in your itinerary. Ferries are easier to access.

Car Rental

For long trips, where you may want to stop, renting a car can be convenient and helpful. It is not impossible to drive in Japan. It is fairly reasonable to rent a car. However, in major cities, it is more affordable to go with a train, bus, or taxi.

In Japan, you need an international driver's permit to rent a vehicle. You also need to be 18 years at least, as this is the age you need to be as a Japanese citizen to drive.

For fueling your rental, there are self-service locations with Japanese only menus. Full-service locations do require that you have some simple language skills.

Chapter 6: Weather

Japan is not as southern as most Asian islands, which translates into a variety of weather. Certain prefectures in Japan have four seasons. To give you a highlight, you should understand when to travel if you are going as a tourist. For those living in Japan as an English teacher, with the military, or in other positions, the weather is not controllable and perhaps just helpful to understand.

Average Temperatures Per Month

January is a cold month, with a high precipitation rating depending on where you travel. For example, Tokyo is 50 degrees F on average, with 36 degree F temperatures at night, and 15 percent chance of rain or snow, with 75% of the days being sunny. Sapporo is 30 degrees during the day, 18 degrees F at night, with 60 percent chance of rain or snow, and 35 percent of sunny days.

Despite the colder weather, New Year is a significant travel season for international and domestic travel. Many of the restaurants, shops, and tourist locations close from December 29 to January 4, but the weather is more often sunny in the main tourist places like Tokyo and Osaka. It is in the north that you will find snow and plenty of it during January.

February is about the same as January, while March begins to change, with more rain, and an adjustment towards warmer temperatures in Tokyo. April is even better with the average temperature in the high 60s, with more rain and fewer sunny days. Spring is when you want to see the fantastic cherry blossoms, plum trees, and Sakura flowers. Naha is the hottest location being in Southern Japan, so if you want beach weather go there.

May, June, and July start bringing more of the cities into the 70s and 80s, with a higher chance of precipitation, but also more sunny days than the spring. July is also known for its festivals and fireworks. Mount Fuji is available for climbing and beach holidays in Okinawa are busy.

August supplies temperatures in the 80s and 90s, with the sunniest days out of the year. September is still warm, but it is typhoon season. You may want to avoid Kyushu, Okinawa, and Shikoku during August and September due to the typhoons.

October and November are still warm weather months, with half the month filled with sun and low precipitation. December becomes cooler with temperatures in the 30 degrees F to 50 degrees F as the average. Rain is also low, with an increase in the sun.

Autumn colors are best in November. For the best weather, consider December as the month to travel. However, the days are shorter, with early sunsets at about 4:30 pm.

Chapter 7:
Jobs and Cost of Living

Already, the history of Japan in having long work days is known. But, what can you do if you want to move to Japan? What is available? Is the cost of living worth it? You will need these answers to decide if you are ready to live as an expat or temporary employee in Japan.

Cost of Living Explanation

According to statistical websites, Japan's cost of living is 16.41 percent higher than living in the USA. It does not mean all prefectures are the same. The higher cost of living is found in Tokyo and other primary cities. For meals, you can expect that inexpensive establishments will be around $7 to $10 per trip. If you go to a mid-range restaurant expect to pay five times the reasonable location, or $35 to $40. Milk is not a high priority in Japan, so you will spend near $7 for a gallon. Other things like eggs, bread, and rice are closer to a few dollars. For a pound of beef, you should expect to pay $7 or more.

Already you can see differences and what many Japanese focus on for their food staples. There are places you can find more detailed information, but understand that you are going to pay less for local items and common items Japanese use in their cooking than you are going to pay for imported items and things like milk.

Clothing is also highly expensive. For a pair of jeans, you may pay as much as $65 and around $40 for a dress. It will all depend on the brands you wear and if you are willing to shop at the local stores. If you want imports be prepared to pay.

Schooling

For people moving to Japan with children, you should understand that school is free up to a certain point. The school term is a three-term system in most locations, with the year starting in April. The day lasts for six hours, where there is a summer break of six weeks and 2-week breaks between the winter and spring terms. Homework is also provided for these breaks.

Kids are in elementary for six years, junior high for three, and can enroll in high school for three years. High school is not compulsory. If a student enrolls in university, it is four years. Public elementary and middle schools are available without charge. It is possible to use private facilities and like the Western world, pay for the privilege. You do have to pay for lunches whether you send meal or have the school prepare it for your child.

There are personal fees like class equipment and musical instruments children will pay for depending on whether they play an instrument. High school is not free of charge. A public school requires at least 200,000 Yen, and this is not the tuition fee. A student can also go part-time and pay 50,000 Yen. For a private high school, the payments become 600,000 yen. This translates into $1784 per year for a full-time high school student going to a public school. It is not easy to afford that unless the parents can help. Many students are starting to get jobs and go part-time. There has been a rise in numbers of young kids going through high school and university.

School can be challenging for foreigners because of the excessive bullying. It is real, and it does happen to students, even Japanese students. Teachers are also more hands-on with their student's education and in their personal lives to see that they are doing well.

Jobs for Expats

Typically, expats can find jobs temporarily in the schools and companies, where English needs to be taught. Like most countries, Japan requires you to have a high education, with a degree that fits your job seeking level. Corporations may bring you in for your experience in management, but often retail at a lower level is not going to be an acceptable job to get a work visa and permit.

Skills that are not readily accessible in the Japanese community are what you will find available. The work is usually temporary.

Despite the challenges, it is not improbable to obtain a job, but be prepared to experience some trouble fitting in and being respected for your knowledge.

Chapter 8:
Best and Worst

Japanese life is enlightening and enjoyable. Military personnel enjoys their time overseas. But, like any place, there are good and bad aspects.

The Best

- You get to experience a diverse culture, with rules and values that often rise above Western experiences, particularly in the US.
- You can try new foods.
- People are hardworking and serious about their jobs.
- There is time for fitness.
- Entertainment is easy to find.
- Heritage sites are many and exciting to enjoy.
- You can travel throughout the different prefectures with public transportation, enjoying places like Nara, Hokkaido, and Kyoto.
- Japanese are friendly, respectful, and curious helping you to start conversations as a tourist.

- You will get to see the lifestyle of today and how it compares with the past.
- There is plenty to learn.

The Worst

- You better like sushi, otherwise, you may have trouble finding enough food in certain places.
- For expats, there are stigmas, and bullying in schools.
- The cost of living is higher than the US, but rent is better.
- You are required to work long hours, without proper over time or what you are used to for over time.
- You will need to learn the language to survive.
- There are customs that you must follow.

The rules and customs of Japan are not wrong, but they are different. In fact, you will get used to these traditions and understand why they should be adopted in more places around the world.

Etiquette and Customs

Manners are imperative to Japan. People greet by bowing, with a small nod or deep bend at the waist depending on the respect, you want to give. A foreigner can bow with the head, and you are not expected to understand the deep bow. Shaking hands is very uncommon, but some Japanese will initiate it, as a sign of their understanding of Western culture.

You are to remove your shoes in the home and at a ryokan (traditional inns). Some restaurants, temples, and castles also ask that you remove your shoes.

Dining out can be in places with low tables, where you will need to sit on pillows.

Chopsticks are the primary source of utensils.

It is not customary to tip, but you should say "gochisosama deshita" when leaving as a sign of respect and saying thank you for the meal.

Gift giving is common, where you are meant to provide a gift in a set of four. Birthdays and Christmas are not traditional gift-giving times, but there are different occasions when it is necessary.

Can you help me?

If you enjoyed this book, then we really appreciate it if you would post a short review on Amazon. We read all the reviews and your feedbacks will help us improve our future books.

If you want to leave a private feedback, please email your feedback to: feedback@dingopublishing.com

Thanks for your support!

Now, let's continue on next page

Conclusion

Japan is a mixture of old and new traditions, where Buddhism is still the primary practice of religion, and you are expected to bow your head instead of shaking a hand. Assimilating in Japan will require a short period of transition for foreigners working in the country. For visitors, just make sure you follow the basic rules and apologize, first if you feel you may not understand a custom.

Above all, when you travel to Japan enjoy the various sites like the ancient temples, tombs, and historical pagoda structures that are all throughout Kyoto.

If you are visiting for business purposes, it is imperative that you understand the rules of business, which are not included. There are first meetings, subsequent meetings, and the actual business of working with Japanese once you agree to conduct business with each other.

Before you travel, have a handle on basic language needs, such as bathrooms, transportation, and checking in at your hotel. It is a sign of respect to at least attempt a few words to indicate you respect the culture and people.

Have fun on your trip, whether it is business, pleasure, or living there. The Japanese culture teaches us a lot about how a small place can continue traditions, without sacrificing basic human decency.

Before you go

We have a surprise for you!

As a way of saying thanks for your purchase, I'm offering a special gift that's exclusive to my readers.

Claim your bonus from the link below:

http://bit.ly/VBonus1

Another surprise! There are free sample chapters of our **best-selling** books at the end.

Australia: History of Australia by James Walker

North Korea – History of North Korea by Mark Thompson

More books from us

Ramen Noodles Cookbook by Linda Nguyen

Pho Cookbook by Linda Nguyen

Kale Cookbook by Olivia Green

Chia Seeds Cookbook by Olivia Green

Anti-inflammatory Diet For Beginners by Jonathan Smith

Intermittent Fasting by Jonathan Smith

HIIT – High Intensity Interval training by Joshua King

Anti-cancer diet by Olivia Green

Bonus #1

Sample chapters of Australia – History of Australia book.

Introduction

For generations in schools, both in Australia and in many other parts of the western world, students were taught that the first settlers in Australia were the British. This has been shown to be incorrect. One reason is that on the coast of Western Australia DNA testing has proved that there is European ancestry in some of the Aboriginal tribes in both the northern and southern areas.

In fact, there are a number of aboriginal people living in these isolated areas who have blue eyes, some with blond hair and some even have very fair skin coloring. These people can trace their parentage back to times before the first know landing of Europeans in Australia, so the question is, how did they manage to have European ancestry. Nobody knows, although there is a lot of speculation it may have been early sea travelers like the Vikings 700 years before Captain Cook sailed into Botany Bay in 1770.

Chapter One:
A Brief History of Australia

The first humans to discover Australia travelled there by sea around 60,000 years ago. Being mainly nomadic and living from hunting as well as gathering their food they were able to easily adapt to living in almost all parts of Australia.

Early in the fifteenth century, many European countries were exploring the world looking for new lands and riches such as gold and other precious metals.

The Dutch were one of the most adventurous and aggressive of the early explorers; they believed there were many areas in the southern hemisphere where gold could easily be found.

The first of the Dutch sailors in these southern waters, William Jansz in 1606 discovered Cape York in what is now known as Queensland Australia. When they landed, they thought the place was very inhospitable with its snakes, large crocodiles, sharks and stinging jellyfish. The natives they encountered were also not very friendly, so he did not stay long.

Around the same time other Dutch ships were sailing the Australian waters, they reported that most of the west and northern areas were barren and lacked water making them of little economic value to the Dutch. They named the country New Holland and "Terra Australis Incognita" which translates to Unknown Southern Land.

Willem Janszoon was the first (Dutch) European to document his meetings with the local Aboriginal People as he sailed and charted the east coast in his ship "The Dyfken".

It has been estimated that there were at least 54 European ships from a number of different countries visiting Australia between 1606 and 1770. One of these ships was captained by Able Tasman, a ship like many of the ships sailing the southern hemisphere that time, owned by the Dutch East Indies Company.

Able Tasman charted much of the coastline of Australian and later, had several areas named after him including the Tasman Sea and Tasmania

The famous English man, Captain James Cook in his sailing ship "Endeavor" mapped the east coast of Australia and then on the 22 of August 1770 he claimed the east coast of

Australia for the English King, George III and named it New South Wales

Captain Cook then sailed southeast and discovered New Zealand and many of the islands of the South Pacific.

Other explorers such as the English mariners Bass and Flinders made detailed maps of the Australian coast with the help of the French mariner Baudinmd. They discovered that Tasmania was a separate island.

There were a multitude of explorers all around Australia at that time and many areas have been named after them. Some well-known examples of this are; Arnhem Land, Torres Strait, Tasmania, Dampier Sound, the Furneaux Islands, La Perouse and Cape Frecinyet.

Chapter Two:
The First Fleet and the Start of a New British Colony

When the first British immigrants arrived in Australia they were not properly prepared or equipped for living in

Australia, they expected conditions to be similar to the areas they had left in England. They came in 11 ships commanded by Captain Arthur Phillip that held a total of 13500 people including the crew and passengers.

They landed at Botany Bay between the 18th and 20th of January 1788 and found the area was not suitable for building their settlement. The seeds and plants they had brought with them did not suit the climate and so they relocated to Camp Cove Port Jackson on 26th Jan 1788

Captain Arthur Phillip was made Governor and had instructions to build the first British Colony in New South Wales. He found that they were totally unprepared and had neither the equipment or food supplies needed. They made friends with the local Aboriginal people, started trading with them for basic food and with them, developed farms in the Parramatta region about 25 kilometers inland on more suitable land.

When the second fleet arrived with badly needed new supplies and equipment in 1790 it made things much easier for the struggling first colony.

This second fleet was supposed to bring new settlers and convict labor for the colony, but it was known as the "Death Fleet" because the living conditions during the trip were so bad that 278 of the crew and convicts died on the voyage.

The colony had a difficult time because of the climatic conditions they encountered, lack of provisions and basic food stocks. There were also social problems because at that time in the colonies there were four times as many men as women.

Contact and Colonization

The area of Albany was claimed in 1791 by George Vancouver creating a new British colony in Western Australia for King George 111.

Generally, when the first European explorers arrived in Australia and met with the native or Aboriginal people they found them to be friendly and easy to get on with.

Once they managed to communicate and started trading they found the Aboriginals were very interested in some western items like axes, knives and shiny trinkets. The aboriginal people also liked blankets, but were not very interested in clothes, as they did not wear them.

Governor Phillip was very active in gaining the help of the Aboriginal people for farming, hunting, fishing and trading. They at first were very cooperative, but then when they discovered the settlers were taking their land and excluding them, they became understandably hostile.

There were many confrontations when the aboriginals were either just killed or driven away from the areas being farmed and settled by the colonists. In the Sydney area the "Eora" clan and their leader Pemulwuy of the Bidjigal planned and undertook a series of attacks designed to frighten off the settlers between 1790 and 1810.

The Governor responded by placing a bounty on any aboriginal found in the areas where the colonies were located, dead or alive. The government also gave out licenses to shoot Aboriginals on sight, which caused any remaining Aboriginals to flee the area. The last of these licenses was revoked in 1957.

Chapter Three:
New South Wales, The Law and Land

New South Wales started as a penal colony in 1788 and remained that way until 1823. Its population was made up of a small number of free settlers that came on the early ships, but mainly convicts, their guards and marines as well as some of their wives. A few lucky convicts became guards because of their good behavior, this was unpaid, but they had their sentences reduced. Once the convicts had served their prison time they were released and allowed to settle where they chose.

The British government established in 1823 the first New South Wales Parliament, first they set up a Legislative Council and then the Supreme Court. Under an act of The English Parliament in London; it was known as the 1823 New South Wales Act (UK). This was the very first step to creating a new Government in Australia. It gave the free people and the convicts both criminal and civil courts to air their grievances.

The indigenous land owners were not recognized by the government until the 1830s when there were two land treaties signed between John Batman and the Kulin people for 600,000 acres of land between Melbourne and the Bellarine Peninsula.

This, for the first time, acknowledged that the Aboriginal people owned the land and had the right to sell it. Sir Richard Bourke, the NSW Governor was not happy about this arrangement as it would set a precedent that others would follow. He issued a proclamation that stated that all the land of Australia belonged to no one before the British crown had taken possession of it. It further stated that all land now belonged to the British Crown.

The British Colonial Office agreed with Governor Bourke and issued another Proclamation that stated that "Any person found in possession of any land they did not have the express permission of the government to occupy would be treated as trespassers."

They also stated that the crown owned all the land claimed by Captain Cook on 22 August 1770, under instructions from King George III of England. Before this claim, the land was owner-less, even though the "House of Commons" had recognized in 1873 that Aboriginal occupants had the legal rights to their land.

The law stated that in order for anyone to claim a title to any land they first had to purchase it from the government whether they were Aboriginal or from another country.

This ruling from 1830 was used in the Australian courts until 1992 when the High Court recognized the traditional land ownership and rights of the Australian Aboriginal in the "Mabo" Lands Rights Case in 1992.

In 1861 The Crown Land Act permitted any person, regardless of their country of origin to select and get a title to a section of Crown land of up to 320 acres of to settle on.

The conditions were that a suitable deposit had to be paid and they had to occupy (live on) the land for at least three years.

This Crown Land Act had the effect of limiting the Aboriginal people's right of access to these newly formed pastoral and farm lands. Up until this time much of this land was the traditional home and hunting lands of the Aboriginals who lived in those areas.

This opening up of the land to new settlers resulted in many conflicts between the various groups who were competing for the land. This included the new landowners, the Aboriginals who were living there, various squatters and the government agents who were charged with selecting who could claim the land titles.

Huge areas of what was vacant land was now being claimed, this caused many disputes and resulted in a relatively large number of people becoming fugitives from the law. Some, because they missed out on getting a property, turned to a life of crime, such as the famous bushranger and highwayman "Ned Kelly".

Other people tried to use elaborate schemes to swindle others from their legally obtained property, they were known as bushwhackers.

Despite all the problems people faced, the former penal colony of New South Wales grew and prospered. The area where the first British Colony started, The Port Jackson Settlement is now Sydney, which has become Australia's largest city.

****End of sample chapters****

Australia: History of Australia by James Walker

Bonus #2
Sample chapters of <u>North Korea – History of North Korea</u>

Chapter One: Japanese Territory

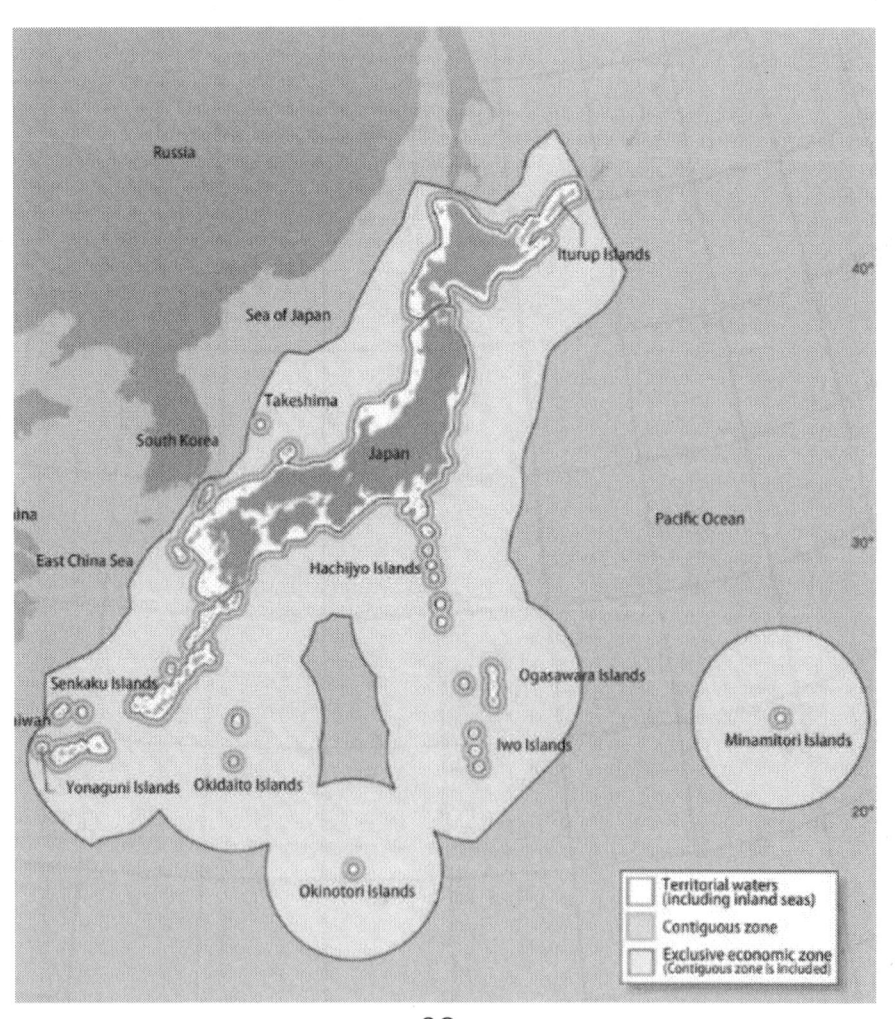

In our modern world, which is currently so widely afflicted by conflicts and territorial disputes, North Korea seems to frequently slip under the radar when it comes to being seen as a threat to global peace. Every now and then, she becomes the subject of public attention, when she tests a nuclear device or experiences a mass famine, but in general, much of what happens in that country goes unreported and unnoticed. There is no major battle being fought there and there are not thousands of refugees fleeing across her borders, so it is easy to assume that, though all is not well, no real disaster looms from that quarter. That blinkered thinking may just prove to be a major shortcoming. Like it or not, that tiny country is on the brink of becoming a player in the deadly nuclear weapons arena, and at the same time her leader feels he has a major axe to grind with the West. It is high time we sat up and paid a little more attention to this troubled state.

Although many analysts tend to view the history of North Korea, as we now know it, as starting from the end of World War II, it is impossible to really understand that country's past without looking a little further back in time. In 1910, Korea was annexed by Japan in what would later be seen to be a violation of international law. The Japanese were quick to take measures to repress local culture and trade. At the same time, they began large scale industrialization projects but these were all aimed at taking wealth from the Koreans and moving it into the hands of the Japanese. Because of the rugged nature of the country, much of the early industrialization took place in the north whilst the south was seen more as an agricultural region with its flatter landscape and gentler climate. This action would become an important factor when the north and south were to split up in the decades to follow.

By 1919, the Japanese occupation had caused enough resentment among the local population for them to start expressing their discontent. This at first took the form of industrial action and rallies but on March the 1st of that year, Korean leaders assembled and signed a declaration of independence. Unsurprisingly, they were immediately arrested, but anti-Japanese resistance quickly increased. In the months that followed, the Japanese cracked down hard on any acts they perceived as insurrection and killed more than 7000 Koreans. The uprisings and resistance took on a new dimension. The resistance leadership fled to Shanghai where they amalgamated to form the Provisional Government whose main role was to co-ordinate confrontation with the occupational forces. Their Chinese hosts were locked in their own battle with Japan and were unable to offer much assistance to the Koreans but they did provide a base from which to operate and allow them to set up an army. At the same time the West, and America in particular, did little to assist them in their struggle. This lack of support would later be remembered.

Chapter Two:
After The Japanese

During World War II, both Russia and the US moved into Korea. Soviet troops now occupied the north whilst the south was occupied by US troops. By agreement of the two occupying forces the country was split directly along the 38th parallel. This left the US in possession of Seoul which was the Korean capital. The Russians worked with an existing form of

Peoples Committees and allowed a great deal of autonomy. The Americans, fearing a Soviet Dominance of the region took a much more hands on approach. During this period Kim Il-Sung returned to Korea after training with both the Chinese and Russians and gaining combat experience against the Japanese.

The Russians and Americans tried to negotiate an agreement on the future of the peninsular but no agreement could be reached. Eventually the US took the problem to the UN who ordered that elections should take place. The Soviets immediately objected and so, in 1948, elections were held in the south which saw the creation of the Republic of Korea. In response, the north elected a Supreme People's Assembly and declared a Democratic People's Republic of Korea with Kim as supreme commander. The soviets recognized the DPRK while the UN recognized the Republic of Korea. The seeds of division were then sown.

Despite the fact the both the US and the Soviets had political motives for acquiring influence on the Korean peninsula, both sides were still recovering from World War II and neither party was keen to commit troops to the region. The Russians began withdrawing their own troops shortly after the end of the war and the US had all but a token number of troops out by 1949. Kim meanwhile was pushing both the Chinese and the Russians for support for his dream of a united Korea. He had a well trained and equipped army who had seen plenty of combat against the Japanese and against Chinese nationalists. The south on the other hand, found themselves with a relatively small and underequipped army.

Skirmishes between the two fledgling states started almost immediately along the 38th parallel. Kim ll-sung was constantly pressing both the Chinese and Stalin to support him in an invasion. At first both of these China and Russia were un-anxious to fully commit to a full scale conflict but Kim soon managed to gather support. This now paved the way for the Korean War.

Chapter Three:
The Korean War

Although the Koreans may have been fighting for their own interests, for the US and the Soviets, the war that would take place in Korea was all about the Cold War. The ideologies of communism and western capitalism were almost bound to collide at some point. Korea provided the ideal battle ground for the conflicting political viewpoints. In 1950, Kim Il-Sung launched a series of attacks all along the 38th parallel. He used an incident that was supposed to have taken place in Ongjin on the 25th of June as justification for the invasion. Claiming that the South Koreans had launched an unprovoked attack at Ongjin, he launched a full scale invasion of the south.

His Soviet equipped army very quickly overran most of the peninsular driving the weak and inexperienced South Korean army and the small American contingent far to the south east of the peninsular. He captured the capital Seoul and this forced the South Korean government under Syngman Rhee to flee. The American forces and what remained of the South Korean defenses managed to hold onto a small section of ground known as the Puson Perimeter.

For the US, there was little regional or territorial gain to be had by entering a war in Korea but the invasion took place at a time when it was not domestically acceptable to be seen to be soft on communism. As a result, the famed General MacArthur, overseeing the occupation of Japan at the time was called on to retake South Korea. At the same time, the United Nations was pressured by both the US and NATO to condemn Kim's actions. This resulted in them also having to send troops to the tiny Pusan area.

MacArthur's actions were characteristically swift and daring. He quickly launched a large scale amphibious raid on the west side of the peninsular from where he began a pincher like attack on the North Koreans. It was not long before he recaptured Seoul and began to chase the North Korean Army back across the 38th parallel. The General was ordered to withdraw on several occasions but his military confidence, public support at home and his ego meant that he could push the North Koreans right up to the Manchurian border which immediately triggered a counter action by the Chinese. The war came at a time when the West had witnessed a communist takeover in China and a co-responding expansion of the Iron Curtain in eastern Europe and so the American public were in no mood to back down to communist expansion elsewhere.

President Truman had hoped that this would be a small war that would end quickly but MacArthur's defiance of orders opened the door for the People's Republic of China to secretly send an army into North Korea at the Yalu River thus escalating what might have been a small scale conflict. Eventually Truman was forced to remove MacArthur from the field and replace him with Lt General Ridgway. It was a very unpopular move in America, with MacArthur being seen as a war hero, and it nearly cost Truman his Presidency.

Ridgway set up a series of fortifications along the 38th parallel and from there was able to hold the communist forces at bay. Negotiations then started between the two sides but they were long and protracted and neither side was keen to be seen to give ground. During this period, the American's engaged in intensive bombing programs, targeting infrastructure in the north. In years to come this would greatly weaken that countries ability to re-establish itself.

Finally, in 1953, a tentative peace agreement was achieved that effectively re-established the status quo that had existed prior to the North Korean invasion. A demilitarized zone was set up between north and south but that term is somewhat misleading as one million troops now face each other across the 38th parallel. At the same time it created added friction to the already volatile cold war. For the Americans it was also the first war that they had ever entered without winning and this would have a deep psychological impact. The effect was profound enough for the US to quadruple its future military spending.

The Korean War, coming so close on the heels of World War II, sometimes tends to get somewhat forgotten in the annals of history. In terms of loss of life, it was devastating. The US lost 36 thousand men with a further 100 thousand injured. The South Koreans lost 217 thousand soldiers and over a million civilians. North Korea and China lost over a million troops and 600 thousand civilians. In total the Americans spent $67 billion on their war effort.

That often under reported war played a critical part in the mindset that today lingers in modern North Korea.

Chapter Four:
KIM Il-SUNG

No one played a greater role in the history of North Korea than Kim Il-sung. He established a dynasty of leaders with an almost cult like status that continue to have a huge influence over the state. He was born in the north of Korea in April 1912, and was given the name Kim Song-ju. His father was a protestant leader in a Presbyterian church. One of the few western organizations that had made any inroads into Korean society was that of Christian missionaries. For some years, whilst the Japanese were in control of the peninsula, Christianity managed to have a secure toe hold. Kim's family were never poor but were also never far from the door of poverty. Like many Korean families they held a deep resentment toward the Japanese and whilst Kim was still young the family crossed the border to take up residence in Manchuria. This was quite common at the time and it has not been definitely established if the family were fleeing after having taken some sort of action against the Japanese or if they were simply fleeing famine. It seems likely, however, that his mother at least, had played some form of activist role.

Kim spent most of his formative years in Manchuria but was quickly drawn into the clandestine world of anti-Japanese activism. He also abandoned the feudal system that his family had followed for generations in favor of Communism which soon drew him to the attention of the Chinese authorities. His activities led to him spending several months in prison. From 1931 to 1935 he was a member of various anti-Japanese guerrilla groups. When the Chinese invaded Manchuria in 1931 tensions against them rose and in 1935 Kim joined the Northeast Anti-Japanese United Army which was effectively a wing of the Chinese Communist Party. He came to the attention of his commanding officer Wei Zengmin who was to have a profound influence on him. Wei reported directly to Mao Zedong and his favorable reports about Kim assured the young man of a quick rise to prominence. In the same year Kim changed his name to Kim

Il-sung which means 'Kim become the sun.' By 1937, he was commander of the 6th Division at only twenty four years old.

He became famous among the Chinese guerrillas for his fighting ability and the Japanese referred to him as the 'Tiger.' Much of this part of his life would later be used as propaganda material on which his cult status was to be established so it is sometimes difficult to separate fact from fiction. By 1937, he was the only commander from the 1st Army left alive and was forced to flee and lead his troops into the Soviet Union to escape the advancing Japanese. He became a Major in the Soviet Red Army and served in that role until the end of World War II.

In August of 1945 the Red Army declared war and crossed into Korea under the Communist leadership of Lavrenity Beria who had been instructed by Stalin to be on the lookout for a potential leader for the country. He had several meetings with Kim and although he was impressed by the young exile the Soviets still planned to put Cho Man-sik into power. At that stage the commander of Soviet forces on the peninsula was General Terentii Shtykov and he favored Kim over the less pliable Cho. He effectively paved the way for Kim to become the Chairman of the Provisional People's Committee of North Korea. Though this would make Kim the most powerful man in Korea he was still answerable to the General and his Soviet commanders.

Kim was quick to start creating the Korean People's Army. He surrounded himself with a cadre of experienced fighting men who had spent years in covert combat with the Japanese. Stalin provided the KPA with the latest tanks and artillery and they were given further training to augment the guerrilla tactics they were already familiar with. They were also provided with aircraft and sent men to be trained as pilots. All of this would provide Kim with a powerful force with which to invade the south in later years.

It was Kim who pushed for the invasion of the south. The Soviets were reluctant to enter a conflict that might agitate the west but eventually acquiesced when their intelligence services persuaded Stalin that Truman would not intervene in a war of unification in Korea.

Kim crossed into South Korea in 1950 in a surprise attack that quickly saw his troops take most of that country. Unlike the Soviets in the North, the US had done little to establish a credible fighting force in South Korea. Their army was quickly overwhelmed and, along with the small US contingent that remained in the country, were forced to free to a small area in the south of the peninsula. When Truman sent General MacArthur to reclaim the south, it came as quite a surprise to both Kim and his Soviet backers. Kim was quickly driven back as far as the Manchuria border and it was only fear that the Americans would have a strong hold right on their doorstep that persuaded the Chinese to reluctantly enter the fray. The Russians stayed out of the war but lent material and tactical support. As the war intensified the Chinese began to play an ever increasing role and Kim found himself being pushed to the side. He was already suspicious of the Chinese and now became desperate for some sort of a treaty that would see him restored to power in North Korea. His dreams of a united Korea would have to be put on hold.

Eventually an agreement was reached which saw the 38th parallel established as a demilitarized zone and Kim was back in power in the north again. There were more than 2.5 million people killed during the war and North Korea, which had once been the most prosperous part of the peninsula, had been devastated by bombing. Kim was still able to portray his return to power as a victory and his influence over the country would begin in earnest. He set about ridding himself of internal opposition and at the same time began building relationships with many of the newly created communist countries of Eastern Europe.

The dream of a united Korea was never far from his mind and he encouraged regular guerrilla attacks across the Demilitarized Zone against both American and South Korean forces. In 1968, his navy even managed to capture the spy ship USS Pueblo along with its crew. The Pueblo incident turned into a major headache for the US administration. The navy ship was captured along with eighty two of the crew. Two had already been killed during the capture. The North Koreans claimed the ship was in their territorial waters and was spying on them. The United States claimed that it was well clear of their waters with orders to monitor Soviet submarines. The crew were held for eleven months in total and during that time they were starved, beaten and tortured. Eventually the Americans negotiated their release but with considerable loss of face to themselves. It is likely that more aggressive action would have been taken had the Vietnam War not been raging on the horizon. Kim used the incident for propaganda purposes and to further bolster his cult status. The Pueblo was never returned and is now a museum in North Korea. For many years it was believed that it was the Soviets who were really behind the Pueblo affair but subsequent information seems to indicate that the North Koreans had acted of their own volition and that this damaged Kim's relationship with that state.

Kim's relationship with the army was strong after his military career and this ensured that his reign would go unchallenged. In 1972, he gave up the title of premier and instead became President of North Korea which was basically simply a titular change. In 1980, he declared that his son would be his next successor which laid the groundwork for the first patriarchal handover in the communist world.

Throughout his time in power, Kim cultivated a close relationship with the military and developed his image to that of an almost god like status with the people. Information was strictly controlled and with no access to what was going on in the outside world it became relatively easy for Kim to direct the way in which he was perceived. There are over five hundred statues of him in the country and his photograph is everywhere. He is still referred to as the Eternal President or the Great General.

There are many myths surrounding him and many of these were generated by the powerful state propaganda machine. They vary from his having been a great and fearless fighter who virtually singlehandedly drove out the Japanese, to his having scored eleven holes in one on his first ever round of golf. The people are also convinced that they are the happiest and best off people on earth and that any woes that befall the country are as a result of counter revolutionary tactics of a jealous West. America in particular is portrayed as an enemy of the state. His birthday remains a public holiday in North Korea and is called the "Day of the Sun".

He died on the 8th of July 1994 from myocardial infarction and was eighty two years old at the time. His death was followed by ten days of national mourning and his funeral was attended by more than a million people who lined the streets for the funeral procession. Many of the mourners were in tears and some even became hysterical. His body is now in the mausoleum at the Kumsusan Palace of the Sun where it remains in a glass coffin for viewing purposes.

Kim Il-sung will undoubtedly be remembered as the founding father of North Korea. His ability to play the Chinese off against the Russians in order to obtain his own objectives are now legendary though were done subtly enough at the time that he was able to keep both states as backers. To the outside world he may be seen as a dictator and even a murderer but to the North Korean's themselves he was a hero. This is particularly true of the modern generation. They have grown up being told by the state that this man was virtually a god, and whilst they may secretly have questions about his successors, the first of the Kim's will continue to be an icon of freedom from oppression by the Japanese and the US.

Chapter Five:
KIM JONG-IL

Several years prior to his death, Kim Il-sung began grooming his third son Kim Jong-Il to take over leadership of the country. From the early 1980s onwards, he had already started being placed in positions of prominence and was seen and accepted to be the heir apparent to his father. For some time prior to the death of Il-sung, the old man's health had deteriorated and the running of the country was effectively in Jong-Il's hands. His father was not seen for such a long time prior to his death that there was considerable speculation that he was already dead but that speculation was laid to rest when Il-sung made a very public state appearance.

After the Great Leaders death the younger Kim took on many titles in the same manner as his father had done. Along with other titles he became General Secretary of the Workers Party of Korea, Chairman of the National Defense Commission and Supreme Commander of the Korean People's Army, the fourth largest standing army in the world. The North Korean population would refer to him as 'Dear Leader' to differentiate him from his father who they referred to as 'Great Leader.' That love of grandiose titles never diminished and in 2009 Kim amended the constitution to declare himself Supreme Leader of the Democratic Republic of Korea.

Jong-Il was born in Russia in 1941. Like many young communists, he was educated with a strong bias toward politics and Marxist political theory. He will have returned to Korea at the age of four when his father triumphantly declared victory over the US and South Koreans. Even prior to coming to power, the party began building a cult like status around him that followed closely that of his father. He recognized very quickly that his power lay in his strong relationship with the military and he emphasized the national policy of Songun that his father introduced. The policy basically promoted that the army came first in national priority and it was heavily supported in national propaganda programs which make up so much of the life of North Korean people. The people were encouraged to believe that the army was to receive precedence over all other national policies including economic decisions.

It is difficult to over-emphasize the cult personality that was built around the second Kim. His father had a guerrilla war to build his persona around whereas Jong-Il had less to work with. He had, however, inherited a totalitarian state and as someone who once oversaw the Propaganda and Agitation Department he knew how to build an image. All artists and musicians were encouraged to promote him and myths were created. It was reported that his birth was foretold by a swallow and that on the day of his birth a double rainbow hung over the revered Mount Paekdu. In his authorized biography, it states that he composed six operas and has a library of over 20 000 films. Despite the state apparatus that went into building his almost mythical status many outside observers still believe that while his father was genuinely adored, the second Kim is revered out of fear.

Jong-Il was the ultimate dictator and would brook no opinions that were different to those of his own. He was said to be both egotistical and arrogant. He was also deeply suspicious of almost everyone around him. These personality traits did not combine well with a renowned inability to manage economic affairs.

North Korea has very little farming land and only eighteen percent of the country is suitable for economic activity. Under the Japanese there had been a great focus on industrialization in the North and this made that region wealthier than the more agriculturally orientated south. The Americans bombed most of the industrial bases and factories out of existence but Kim Il-sung had the support of Russia to bolster his economy. Jong-Il was less fortunate than his father in many respects. The south was now seeing huge US funded development which helped the South Koreans establish strong technology businesses. This combined with their ability to produce food soon pushed them into a far more comfortable financial position than that of North Korea.

The collapse of the iron curtain saw North Korea lose its biggest trading partner and at the same time relations with the Chinese deteriorated in response to their recognition of South Korea. Both China and Russia were now looking to improve relations with the wealthy south. The "Dear Leader's" problems were further exacerbated by large scale flooding that took place in 1995 and 1996 followed by a drought. Combined with mismanagement the country saw a devastating famine. External estimates put the death toll for the famine at 2000 000 people but that figure was never admitted to by the regime. In response, Kim strengthened his relationship to the army who he recognized both as his only support against domestic uprising and international threats.

In part, it was this disastrous combination of economic crises that propelled the North Korean nuclear programs. Kim understood that having a nuclear capability would give him both military and economic clout from which to lever his weak position. As early as 1994 the Clinton administration agreed to supply fuel oil and economic aid in return for the freezing and dismantling of North Korea's nuclear weapons policy. For a while, it even began to look as though North Korea would once again enter the world of international acceptance. There were talks between North and South Korean leaders and families who had been separated by the Demilitarized Zone for decades began to be allowed brief visits. Trade deals were mentioned and the future outlook showed a brief glimmer of light.

In 2002, the CIA produced reports that the north were going ahead with a uranium enrichment plan. The then President, George W. Bush, was quick to revoke the 1994 agreement put in place by the Clinton administration, and furthermore, he declared that North Korea was part of the "axis of evil" and added it to the US terrorist nations list. It took until 2003 for the north to admit to the enrichment program and they were quick to point to Bush as the reason they had once more started work on a military nuclear capability. Chinese brokered talks proved unfruitful. The Bus government insisted that no face to face talks would take place until North Korea dismantled its nuclear facilities which that country refused to do. They pointed to the strong US military presence in South Korea and remained adamant that they needed a nuclear deterrent as part of their defense structure. In 2006 they proudly announced their first successful underground nuclear detonation. At around the same time the CIA were reporting that they believed Kim was in possession of at least two function able nuclear weapons. Suddenly the world began to sit up and pay attention to North Korea.

Whilst this was all going on rumors began to surface as to Kim's poor health. A Japanese publication published an article in 2008 in which it alleged that Kim had been dead since 2003 and that a double had been standing in in his place at public events. Speculation became rife but in a country as strictly controlled and secretive as North Korea it was difficult to get confirmation one way or another. To add further to the confusion, it appeared that there was no obvious successor to take over as supreme leader. His sons did not seem to be interested in taking on the mantle and the world began to wonder if the country would be trapped in a power vacuum that could spiral into chaos.

In 2009 Jim Jong-Il announced that his son Kim Jong Un would succeed him. On December the 17th of 2011 it was announced that the "Dear Leader" was dead. He was reported to have died whilst carrying out his work duties from a heart attack. Once again the streets were thronged with wailing people mourning the loss of their beloved leader. It is difficult to tell exactly who his heirs were. At the time of his death he apparently had three wives, three sons and three daughters. Other reports place the number of his children at closer to seventy and allege that many of them are still accommodated in villas dotted about the country. He was known to lead a playboy lifestyle and so it is unlikely that the truth will ever be fully revealed.

**** End of sample chapters ****

North Korea – History of North Korea by Mark Thompson

Thanks again for purchasing this book.

We hope you enjoy it

Printed in Great Britain
by Amazon